All Scripture references taken from the KJV of the Holy Bible, unless otherwise indicated.

UNAUTHORIZED USE

Dr. Marlene Miles

Freshwater Press 2024
Freshwaterpress9@gmail.com

ISBN: 978-1-963164-54-1

Paperback Version

Copyright 2024, Dr. Marlene Miles

All rights reserved. No part of this book may be reproduced, distributed, or transmitted by any means or in any means including photocopying, recording or other electronic or mechanical methods without prior written permission of the publisher except in the case of brief publications or critical reviews.

Table of Contents

- The Natural Use 4
- The Golden Calf 8
- Unnatural Use 12
- Golden Implements 18
- Marriage Bed Undefiled 19
- Broken Down For Parts 22
- One Unauthorized Person 25
- Sexual Rights 32
- Marriage Ritual Violation 41
- Ancestral Marriage Violations 45
- Ask 47
- Masturbation is Unauthorized 52
- Sex Magic 59
- I Said It's Golden 65
- Unless You Are In Christ 71
- *Dear Reader:* 88
- Other books by this author 89

UNAUTHORIZED USE

The Natural Use

For this cause God gave them up unto vile affections: for even their women did change the natural use into that which is against nature:

And likewise also the men, leaving the natural use of the woman, burned in their lust one toward another; men with men working that which is unseemly, and receiving in themselves that recompence of their error which was meet.

And even as they did not like to retain God in their knowledge, God gave them over to a reprobate mind, to do those things which are not convenient;

Being filled with all unrighteousness, fornication, wickedness, covetousness, maliciousness; full of envy, murder, debate, deceit, malignity; whisperers,

Backbiters, haters of God, despiteful, proud, boasters, inventors of evil things, disobedient to parents,

Without understanding, covenant breakers, without natural affection, implacable, unmerciful:

Who knowing the judgment of God, that they which commit such things are worthy of death, not only do the same, but have pleasure in them that do them.(Romans 1:26-32)

When God created man He said, *It is good.* God did not say it is vile or it is reprobate. He said, *It is good.* Man was designed and also wired a certain way, in the image and likeness of God. But like a bad computer program it was all corrupted when man was still corruptible. Now it is on man to work to become uncorrupted again, but some take pleasure in this corruption.

The chapter starts out with people who have forgotten God and have changed the use of one another sexually. From there the spiral downward is easy. Mostly because when the focus is flesh, the spiral is quick. Once God is out of an equation, mankind usually has no stops. Even though we think the vitality of the flesh means life, the flesh can be a killer. The thing we call flesh, the base, immature, and stubbornly willful side of man can kill. Verse 20 recounts the spiral to include backbiting, hating God, pride, evil imaginings, and disobedience to parents.

Just as the 5th Commandment says to Obey Your Parents in the Lord, and it is the first Commandment with promise, doing the opposite surely brings on the Curse of the Law. Disobeying and disrespecting parents is a deadly sin but those who let the flesh rule their lives will easily do this. They also are dark in their understanding and will break covenant and are without natural affection one to another.

Verse 32 says they know the judgment of God, but they do things worthy of death and take pleasure in doing those things.

Why? The devil's taunt to man has always been to defy death.

Thinking back on my youth and probable ignorance, my own will may have been all that mattered after rebelling from so many years of rules in my parents' house. While still young it is not in the mind of any young person that rules are for your protection and running wild or rampant in the streets or in life is dangerous.

Protection is love; but it may take a while for the average person to realize that. Pray that you do and that your children do before it is too late.

Rules and laws are inconvenient to the rebellious and the willful because they limit. People are savvy enough to realize that they can do a lot with this body that God has given them, but they need foresight, Wisdom and understanding to know that the consequences may be very difficult or devastating. Rules and laws are to inhibit unauthorized use of this body, this soul and this person, but youthful folly wants to rule the day. And, the nights.

The Golden Calf

When the people saw that Moses was so long in coming down from the mountain, they gathered around Aaron and said, "Come, make us gods who will go before us. As for this fellow Moses who brought us up out of Egypt, we don't know what has happened to him."

Aaron answered them, "Take off the gold earrings that your wives, your sons and your daughters are wearing, and bring them to me." So all the people took off their earrings and brought them to Aaron. He took what they handed him and made it into an idol cast in the shape of a calf, fashioning it with a tool. Then they said, "These are your gods, Israel, who brought you up out of Egypt."

When Aaron saw this, he built an altar in front of the calf and announced, "Tomorrow there will be a festival to the LORD." So the next day the people rose early and sacrificed burnt offerings and presented fellowship offerings. Afterward they sat down to eat and

drink and got up to indulge in revelry.
(Exodus 32:1-6)

Sometimes the restlessness in man is because he has run out of things to worship. Man is designed to worship; he will worship something, always. The object of his worship should be Jehovah God. But faithless man goes by sight and will worship things that his eyes see, that his flesh touches, that his mouth tastes, for example.

The restlessness of youth is that the young person has finally gotten away from parents and he wants to find his own way in life. Sometimes that own way is finding his own things to worship. Idols can be anything seen or unseen, anything tangible or invisible. Idols can be within self or outside of self. There are so many pretty, beautiful, nice, and available things to worship if one is carnal and walks by sight. Some worship themselves. Some worship others. Some worship things, stuff and money, for example.

In the Wilderness from the worship of idols the scene quickly devolved into sexual sin. From the unauthorized use of gold, which was a spoil from Egypt, the Israelites created an unauthorized golden calf and began to worship it, then then their "society" spiraled down into sexual promiscuity and sin.

They say that money can burn a hole in some people's pockets, so it seems that these folks just had to use that gold for something. They chose an idol. The gold in their possession, even in their ears may have been screaming at them for worship. After all, there is a *god* of gold. Egyptian gold with its own *gods* may have been demanding worship. Folks, this is why every dollar is not a good dollar. This is why we consecrate gain to the Lord, as soon as possible so the *gods* associated with that money, that we most likely got out of the world doesn't talk us into ungodly things and unauthorized usage.

Idol *gods* talk. Constantly.

Of all people, Aaron, Moses' brother asked for the gold, forged the golden calf, then called for offerings to GOD and said there will be a festival tomorrow. And there was, then they ate and drank and indulged in revelry. The doublemindedness is astounding. But when a person is holding unrighteous mammon, they are likely to do almost anything that mammon or the *spirits* that mammon may travel with suggest.

Unnatural Use

Because of this, God gave them over to shameful lusts. Even their women exchanged natural sexual relations for unnatural use. (Romans 1:26)

Just as Sodom and Gomorrah and the adjacent cities, since they in the same way as these angels indulged in gross immoral freedom and unnatural vice and sensual perversity. They are exhibited in plain sight as an example in undergoing the punishment of everlasting fire. (Jude 1:7)

Spiritually, unnatural use is simply using something in a way that God said don't, or in some other perverse way. Perversions are either suggested or insisted on by entities and *spirits* from the dark kingdom whether folks realize that's where they are getting the idea or not. Natural or normal use has built-in protections. Just as rules and laws are for the protection of those under those rules.

Unnatural use is a free-for-all. According to the passage above the persons doing this will be put to death. Now, in the Garden at Eden, God told Adam and Eve if they ate of that tree they would surely die. God doesn't lie, so they died on the spot. The same applies to these parties if Adam and Eve died (spiritually) on the spot then what the Word says is true. These people who are doing things worthy of death, unless they repent and accept Jesus Christ, they are now dead.

They went into whatever place they went, still alive (possibly and probably) and came out dead. Of course, we don't know without discernment of the Holy Spirit telling us if they were alive when they went in; they could have already been spiritually dead and just going through the motions of ritual sex while killing others who agree to participate with them in their sexual capers.

So two types of spiritually dead: those who know it and those who don't. Those who don't know it are thinking that since they seem to be physically alive that is all that matters. Whether they are spiritually dead is not something they've thought about -- , they are here and in it for the flesh. A good time. The party. The conquest.

Those who are spiritually dead and know it, have cast all caution to the wind; they do not care. They just exist in the moment and give no care to consequences, tomorrow and some don't even care about later on today.

Wrong sex is sex with anyone other than our covenanted, legal spouse. It is also any perversion to what God says sex is for and sex is to be. Any type of wrong sex, especially with someone you are not supposed to sleep with is the same is as though you are accepting the curse of "thou shalt not excel."

- By the Blood of Jesus, please remove and erase the INIQUITY of instability and ***Thou-shalt-not-excel*** for Reuben-like sins and any other sex sins, in the Name of Jesus.

Then there's another group that are spiritually dead and they are physically dead. They are empowered through the evil one to do sexcapades which is a sure-fire way to get demons into humans. While they are distracted in the throes of passion, they have no idea what hit them, or what was taken from them.

When one or two people decide that they are going to use body parts in an unauthorized, unsanctioned way, perversion, abuse, general weirdness that does not lead to be fruitful and multiply--, *anything goes.*

Unauthorized use means that a human, who has all the authority in the Earth that a human has, has opened up the sex gates and the *free for all* has started. It only takes one person to begin an unauthorized use event and every demon that can fit into that room will be there to watch, freak, participate, get involved, give --, take---. And there you thought it was your freaky imagination. No, those are demons giving you those ideas and those thoughts. If they had a body it is what they would do. And/or they want it to be as perverse and abominable to God as possible to bolster their case against you when Satan, the Accuser of the brethren goes to the Throne of God to accuse you before your Heavenly Father of what you did. That is if you either were spiritually alive when you went in, or you still have the hope of redemption by being able to repent and that God would forgive you.

If you are an unrepentant sort roaming about seeking whom you can get with--, you're already spiritually dead, just going through the motions, and working for the devil, most often for free. He won't bother to accuse you to God if he's already got you in his clutches.

Players and OG's are out here in these streets chasing skirt and getting with anyone that they can. Counter to that, there are women out here doing the same thing. Neither group realizes that they've been indoctrinated by the devil, hypnotized as it were, on demonic remote and have ritual sex programming. Those that gotta have it or gotta take it from someone are working for the devil and most don't even realize it. Most don't realize the damage they are doing to others, themselves, and their bloodline, should God not cut off their bloodline.

All these types are spiritually dead until they can meet Christ.

Golden Implements

Rob Blagojevich became too popular for saying, *"I've got this thing and it's golden."*

Too many people behave as if what they have is golden – and it is only flesh. No flesh glories in the presence of God, and no flesh is leaving the planet.

Idols. Idol worship. There is sexual idolatry—people not only worship sex, they worship the sex organs—whether they realize it or not.

When you hear the music, bow. What you bow to, you worship. What is over you, that you allow to be over you, you are worshipping that something.

Marriage Bed Undefiled

The marriage bed is undefiled, at least it should be, and it should remain that way. Careful of what you are doing in that marriage bed, so you do not defile it, so you don't defile your spouse or yourself.

> Just as Sodom and Gomorrah and the surrounding cities, which likewise indulged in sexual immorality and pursued unnatural desire, serve as an example by undergoing a punishment of eternal fire. (Jude 1:7)

Balaam couldn't curse Israel as long as there was no sin in them. They were undefiled. So Balack planned a way to get the men to defile themselves with strange women that he sent in. As soon as the defilement occurred, the curse was able to land, and 24,000 Israelites perished. When one man dies we are diminished, how much more is a people desolated when they lose plague-levels of citizens? These judged and men who died were tempted and defiled their beds with women sent in to do just that. Whether married or not, it was defilement. If they weren't married, they were fornicating and that is still defilement.

The *bed* is not literally the bed; the bed is the use of intimate parts --- when the strange woman comes in, it is to defile the bed, it is to defile the marriage and it defiles the person participating with this defiled agent. When the sex is defiled, the covenant it makes is either negated or also defiled. A defiled bed is a defiled covenant.

When the *strange man* comes in it is to defile the bed and the marriage. Now the individuals can be cursed. And, now the marriage can be cursed, and it most often is as one spouse or the other won't forgive infidelity. Or one spouse will be forgiving and understanding of their own acts of roaming about on the prowl, but they won't forgive their spouse if their spouse falls into that same sin trap.

Sadly, polygamy and infidelity could be in both their bloodlines, whether they've hidden it, or not, and done nothing to address it and here comes the inevitable. A polygamous person doesn't have to have more than one spouse. Polygamy comes in with serial dating and sleeping around. It comes with having baby momma's and baby daddies. A polygamous person can be married to one spouse but is a cheater – a one time cheater or a serial cheater is polygamous.

Especially if the cheated-on person finds out about the others, that's when polygamous witchcraft starts and it is the among the worst kinds of witchcraft that can happen to a people, and their children.

Broken Down For Parts

Women hate being objectified. Don't men also? They should. Objectification of a human is really like breaking it down into the parts you like and ignoring the rest. It is like breaking a person down for parts and ignoring all the other parts of a person, as if that desired part or thing can satisfy.

To the human with a heart of flesh, it is the human touch, the human warmth and human experience that the soul is craving when that person wants to have relations with another. Heartless people don't see it that way.

The sexual implement industry is worth several billion, annually. They sell every kind of gadget to induce sexuality, indiscriminate of couples, marriages, or gender affiliations. Specifically, men and women have been broken down for parts, and those parts are for sale. Facsimiles of sexual organs abound for sale in porn shops and on websites and are accessible by almost anyone anywhere.

No one wants to be objectified, but if a person is in possession of a plastic or silicon body part of another person, that is **unauthorized use.** These objectified "parts" are idols.

Sex with implements and objects is still ungodly, that is not what God intended and it is unauthorized use of yes the fake part, but the person or persons using the "parts" are opening themselves up for demons, *spirit spouses* and all manner of evil from Satan's kingdom.

We are never alone. Never.

If God can't look on what you are doing, because God doesn't hang around evil or run to it, then if what you have chosen to do is sin and it is evil, then His angels are not in your company either. This is when the devil can send in a guardian demon.

Because of fleshly thrills a person can be into all sin and never think that anything is wrong with it. They may think no one knows because the lights were out, the object was hidden in a closet or a drawer, and no one *else* was there.

But, we are never alone--, never. So someone else was there.

The warning of if you do this too much you will go blind does not really apply here. The real warning is if you do this you will die. If you do this, you will die, spiritually. Even while a person may feel exhilarated and very much alive from sin, when you sin, you die. Period.

Someone will always know because we are never alone. Never.

One Unauthorized Person

> Wisdom is better than weapons of war: but one sinner destroyeth much good.
> (Ecclesiastes 9:18)

As far as the devil is concerned, as far as things of the spirit go, if there is one, at least one unauthorized guest at a meeting, an event, even in a bedroom, or bathroom, then the door is open for any and all interlopers. And, he will send in interlopers, pinch hitters, and pro's.

To do what?

Steal sperm.

Evil implantation.

Steal glory, virtue, destinies.

Steal blessings – you know that promotion or that contract you were supposed to get tomorrow. Don't kiss it away tonight "celebrating" prematurely.

What else might the devil be doing? Defiling you. Defiling your partner. Taking worship.

The passage below from Genesis makes being *"wifed"* sound nice, fun and romantic – it's not, especially when it is from the spirit world, which is a definite use that is unauthorized by God. But, saints of God, you have the ability to authorize use of your person. Be wise, do not be foolish and know who you are giving permission to and what you are giving authorization *for*.

> And it came to pass, when men began to multiply on the face of the earth, and daughters were born unto them, That the sons of God saw the daughters of men that they were fair; and they took them wives of all which they chose.
> (Genesis 6:1-2)

This passage is about spirit spouses, and they come to steal kill and destroy. They come to block folks from having a natural spouse by marrying them and becoming their *spirit spouse*. They come to block folks from having natural children, specifically, righteous seed.

Unauthorized use of a body in the natural can always lead to permission given to Satan and any of his horde to come into your life, especially sexually.

If you could go into your own future and look back from the future to where you are now you might better know what the chess move is that the devil would be trying to make against your future, your family, your destiny, your progress, wealth, and bloodline.

He may already have your bloodline in a sling and just coming to re-up evil covenants for another 10 or 14 generations for those who don't believe in God. For those who do, he's trying to re-up evil covenants for another three or four generations. Please note, I did not say years, I said GENERATIONS, and that's a very long time.

So, all it takes is one unauthorized person in the mix. That person could be an unauthorized, *My-Body-My-Life* type who is doing unauthorized, unsanctioned acts.

Such as?

Onan spilled the seed.

If what you are doing will spill seed, God is not in it and He not only does not condone it, but He is also opposed to it. If what you are doing is not human to human, then God is not in it. If what you are doing is not a living, breathing human to living, breathing human, then God is not in it because God does not involve Himself in dead things. My friends, that includes sexual implements which I once heard advertised as a senior relaxation device.

Folks, you do not want a *spirit spouse* as an old person; and sexual implements create unauthorized use of the human body and is a breeding ground for demons who will marry a person and call themselves a *spirit spouse*. It takes a lot to fight *spirit spouse* as a young person, and demons and *spirit spouses* can get more brutal as time goes on. Spirit spouses bring on mystery and chronic diseases. Do you have any idea how long it takes for a senior to get rid of a UTI? *(Do what you will with that information.)*

So, deal with your spiritual stuff now so those demons don't break you down and so you are not suffering in old age and have no way to tell anyone what you're going through at night, for example. And deal with it now and in your youth so your spirit man is built up so you are not helpless as an old person in spiritual matters.

If what you are doing is not *intended* to be fruitful and multiply, is God in it? If what you are doing requires that you hide and sneak, you know good and well that God is not in that. Would God give you a bushel of corn seed and land to plant the seed in and be okay with you going out to the field and burning all the seed? That is certainly unauthorized use of the **seed**.

How many children can you take care of? I don't know, ask God. These are God's children, righteous seed--, how many children can God take care of? If you are conjugating for the purpose of being fruitful and multiplying then God is in that, and God will provide. If you are involved and tangoing with another for the purpose of NO CHILDREN, just for your flesh, God is not in that and it is as though you have predetermined that you will sacrifice a child or children before conception ever happens, if it happens.

- Lord, forgive me for every wrong place I've ever been in.
- Lord, forgive me for all wrong sex I've ever had.
- Lord, forgive me for anything that grieves You, the Holy Spirit –
- Lord, forgive me for every perversion that I've ever participated in, entertained, or

even fantasized about, in the Name of Jesus.
- Lord, forgive me for every unauthorized bed I've ever been in or even *near*, in the Name of Jesus.
- By the Blood of Jesus, please remove and erase the INIQUITY: of instability and ***Thou-shalt-not-excel*** for Reuben-like sins in my life, and for any other sex sins, in the Name of Jesus.

Unstable as water, thou shalt not excel; because thou wentest up to thy father's bed; then defiledst thou it: he went up to my couch.
(Genesis 49:4)

- Lord, remove the curse of death from my life and my bloodline as David and Bathsheba lost their first born due to adultery, whether I knew a sexual partner was married or not.
- Lord, forgive me for any and all unauthorized use of my body, soul, mind, sexual organs, and reproductive system, in the Name of Jesus.
- Lord, forgive me for any and all unauthorized use of another person or persons, whether done soberly, knowingly, or in other states of awareness.

Lord, forgive me and restore that person back to their former glory before I defiled them if that is what I did.
- Lord, forgive me for David sins such as taking a person's only ewe, if I did that. Lord, I repent, please restore their souls, in the Name of Yeshua.
- Lord, forgive me for spilling seed or innocent blood, for sin and murder and murderous thoughts, in the Name of Jesus.
- Lord, forgive me for sacrificing children to the evil *god*, Molech or Chemosh, in the Name of Jesus.
- I am not a pagan, I am not an idolater, I am in Christ, Lord, forgive me, in the Name of Jesus.
- Lord, please forgive me for rape or sexual coercion of anyone at any time, in the Name of Jesus.
- Lord, heal their broken spirit, restore their souls, minds, and body, in the Name of Jesus.
- Lord, wash me clean and purify me with the Blood of Jesus, (X7) Amen.

Sexual Rights

Some may think that rape is the only thing that is defiling. Rape is defiling and foul, because there is no consent, and it seriously violates sexual rights, but all unauthorized use of the human body sexually is defiling. Even spouses have to give consent, else it is rape. Sexual consent and sexual rights are not considered by eloped couples, or shacked-up couples. In those situations, it is as though anything not only goes, anything can come into that relationship in general and in their conjugal relations, specifically.

Spirit spouse sex in the dream relations is rape and its purpose is to control and defile.

Pastor John Cherry, the Lord rest his soul, made impact on me when he said that he and his wife always pray before they have sexual relations. He did not say what they prayed or how they prayed, but I will ask the Holy Spirit for such a prayer because I want that kind of Godly coverage as it relates to sex in the marriage.

Of course, there is no authority for praying before illicit sex, so it has to be sex within the confines of a sanctioned marriage, and only that.

Every living soul should be fruitful and multiply. We all have Divine purpose inherent upon our coming into the Earth. Protocols for marriage need to be followed. Idol *gods* will insist on certain marriage rituals based on culture, geographic location and tradition. Some of those protocols may be that you need to be in the right place to get your spouse because of territorial powers precluding marriage, or requiring that you get permission.

The only way to get out of local, traditional, and territorial rituals and requirements is to be fully in Christ. Are you following the laws of God or are you following tradition, your father's house or the world?

Dowry effects the sale of sexual rights.

I've got this thing, and it is golden, may be the unspoken words of a parent who requires a man to pay the 'bride price" to marry his daughter. Yet that is tradition in some countries.

The proud father of a newborn will almost always say, *She's never going to date or get married.* While that sounds like a spoken curse that will turn that cute baby into a spinster or old maid. But, the sentiment the new dad spoke must be some vestigial impulse or emotion because he is in charge of her sexual rights. In this culture we don't speak this way very often.

Most often a young man may ask for a woman's hand in marriage; he doesn't use the words, *sexual rights.* In a marriage the man owns his wife's sexual rights, and the woman owns the man's. This could be why sexual infidelity is so dramatic and shocking to the cheated-on spouse. He made a vow, a promise and he went back on it. If he or she will do that, what else will they do? Trust is broken.

Jacob never violated marital or sexual rights for Rachel. He went by the book, never risking for a moment losing sexual rights.

> And Jacob said unto Laban, "Give *me* my wife, for my days are fulfilled, that I may go in unto her," (Genesis 29:21)

Jacob worked and worked for Rachel then asked her authority figure, her father, Laban for sexual rights. May I have your daughter's hand in marriage – he didn't ask for the hand, he asked for sexual rights.

> And if a man entice a maid that is not betrothed, and lie with her, he shall surely endow her to be his wife.
>
> If her father utterly refuse to give her unto him, he shall pay money according to the dowry of virgins. (Exodus 22:16-17)

The man in the above verses took a maid's *sexual rights*; they are now married because goes into equals married in the Bible. However, the father has authority to give or refuse sexual rights.

Who has control of your sexual and/or reproductive rights? No one? You don't know who? That could be why you are not married today.

If a parent won't let you go, you may never get married. Or, you may get married, but you won't be happy in marriage. You may end up divorced and back at home with your momma and/or your daddy. We've all seen it too often.

Elopements do not have parental blessings. Sexual rights have not been given to the groom.

Marriage is covenant and it is holy unto the Lord. Marriage is worship unto the Lord. The man who finds a wife finds a good thing and obtains favor from the Lord. Favor is life. If you walk in the favor of God then you will have the favor of men. (Genesis 29:21).

- Lord, in the Name of Jesus, whatever belongs to me that I don't have because I violated a covenant, Blood of Jesus, pay for me, so I may have what is mine. Amen.

If there is a marriage without the proper transfer of sexual rights – the marriage will end up being the punishment. If God is not in a thing, it will devolve into disaster anyway. The spouse will end up being the tormentor. Do not force a marriage else you will end up in forced wedlock instead of holy matrimony.

Getting married without parental blessings brings on curses. It is disrespecting and disobeying parents --, remember the 5th Commandment? If you honor your father and mother you will live long in the Earth and have good success. If you disobey or disrespect your parents you get the opposite.

Your parents eloped so you think it's okay? It's cheaper? You're pregnant and in a hurry? You will get the results your parents got, most likely. In order to get a different and better result, you have to change your foundation.

Strange covenants created by sex before, or after the marriage are such as soul ties, will jack the foundation, and not in a good way. When you jack up your foundation, you mess things up for your children, your' *children's* children, your entire bloodline, really. Idolatry and polygamy ruin foundations.

What is the family history on both sides? What are you marrying into? What might be the spiritual foundation of your children when the two foundations combine? Do you know? You need to know.

Witchcraft drains all the goodness out of a marriage and waits to drain virtues from your children and future generations. Witchcraft defiles the marital bed by suggesting perverse and very perverse things. Man, witches aren't all ugly—she may be the finest, hottest thing you ever saw. You'd better find out if she's a witch before you get your freak on, and/or marry her. Whether married or not, you two could end up pregnant and then what? Male witches are warlocks, ladies--, and they can be fine also; be very discerning.

Parents who don't talk to their children are notorious – some of us don't know if their parents were actually married or not, or just living together. Or, they may have been living apart, yet married. I don't think I'm illegitimate, but I haven't seen my parents' marriage license, and I've heard there was a shotgun involved, but I never met my mother's father, the one who allegedly wielded the shotgun. So let us all pray:

- Lord, in the Name of Jesus, let every curse of the illegitimate birth break against me, in the Name of Jesus.

The child is not illegitimate, the parents, who definitely should know or should have known better, are the illegitimate ones. People of child-bearing age are also at the age of accountability and are responsible to know and follow Biblical laws, and not just let passion flood over them.

Children pray this over your parents:

- Lord, in the Name of Jesus, I forgive my parents for violating or not participating in marriage rituals as they should have or for not being fully in Christ when they conceived, gestated, and gave birth to me. Lord, forgive them and all our ancestors, in the Name of Yeshua.
- Lord, heal them. Heal their emotions, their souls and bodies and let them receive You fully as their Lord and Savior.

Marriage ritual violation can block a bloodline from God for up to 10 generations, unless Jesus gets into the situation.

Having sex with someone transfers **their last 7 demons to you and your last seven to that person**. Sex easily transfers demons. Built in with that are soul ties, broken hearts, possible pregnancy, forced marriages, the curse of thou shalt not excel, poverty, struggles and possible thwarting of destiny. This is all from unauthorized use of people, their bodies and their sexual organs and reproductive system.

A fellow with a bright career was enticed by two sisters, like sirens that he should sleep with them. He did, and lost his lucrative contract the following week and has not even been able to find any job for the past two years, since he slept with those two females. Soul snatchers are real; some are human, some are not even human. Glory snatchers and virtue stealers are all real. Some are in the natural, some are in the dream, but they are assigned against a person and if you authorize yourself for their unauthorized purposes then too bad for you, they do what they want to you and against you.

Better get and stay prayed up.

Married against the parents' will, or without the parental blessing cannot bring blessings; that will bring curses. Unmarried and having sex spreads and collects demons and also brings curses. Married and sleeping around brings curses.

That foundation must be ministered to in prayer and deliverance to change. Being born out of wedlock is a curse, while it's not the child's fault, the child inherits the fall out of it. There's a curse of illegitimate birth.

- In the Name of Jesus, let every curse of illegitimacy, every curse of the illegitimate break against me, in Jesus' Name. Amen.

Marriage Ritual Violation

Marriage ritual violation can block a person from God for up to 10 generations--, unless there's Jesus Christ. It also smacks of Unauthorized Use of body and reproductive parts even by two people who believe they are in love, or **believe they are married**. In the spirit, if you didn't *get married right--*, you are unauthorized and have no permission to have sex with your spouse or reproduce. At least that is how the idols behave and will try to enforce.

In this idol enforcement protocol, if you do nothing and say nothing against it what the idol(s) want will stand.

When we talk about righteous seeds this conversation must be had. Most of us think if the husband and the wife are saved the child will automatically be a righteous seed. Hmmm. It depends on conditions on the ground when and how that child was conceived if a child is righteous seed or not. Are the parents married? Is the marriage bed undefiled? Is God in their union --, yes, their marriage but I mean this actual intimate act of covenant that created this fetus? Had they prayed and asked for the Holy Spirit to be there and with them while they, in love, renewed the conjugal part of their marriage covenant? Were there any other *spirits* in the mix? If one or the other, or both were fantasizing about <u>anything</u> at all while they were in the act, they invited in demons—other *spirits*, and that's not good at all.

Were any conception **rituals** involved? Any of this negates righteous seed.

As the Holy Spirit overshadowed Mary and she became impregnated with Jesus, a truly Righteous Seed, then we want the Holy Spirit to condone our every union with our spouse and be present when we have relations. We want angels to stand guard. We are declaring that this is authorized use and kingly, kingdom business going on.

Behold his bed, which is Solomon's; threescore valiant men are about it, of the valiant of Israel.

They all hold swords, being expert in war: every man hath his sword upon his thigh because of fear in the night.
(Song of Solomon 3:7-8)

What were either and both of these parent's foundations like? Were there any other interferences in there? We are all born in sin and shaped in iniquity, so I can ask were those two *prayed up*? There is probably more to ask about these reproductive conditions that night, or that day, but this is what I share with you at this time.

- Every curse because of any violated marriage ritual, break by the power in the Blood of Jesus. Amen.
- Lord, in the Name of Jesus, uncurse me uncurse me, uncurse my marital destiny.
- UNCURSE my ring finger, uncurse me completely, in the Name of Jesus.
- Lord, I declare that I am divorced from every idol *god*, every *spirit spouse*, in the Name of Jesus. Lord don't let me be a liar,

let this declaration be true, in the Name of Jesus.
- I get rid of every *spirit child* and divorce every *spirit spouse*.
- I disentangled myself from every quantum entanglement, in the Spirit, in the Name of Jesus.
- Lord, don't make me pay for things I don't even know anything about, in the Name of Jesus.
- Lord, don't make me pay for things that I didn't buy, didn't use, didn't get the benefit of, in the Name of Jesus.

Ancestral Marriage Violations

- Lord, anything I have inherited that makes me un-authorizable in the spirit for marriage, break that inherited evil now, in the Name of Jesus.
- Lord, do not make me pay for things just because of my last name and the family I was born into, in the Name of Jesus.
- Lord, do not make me pay for things just because of the bloodline I was born into, in the Name of Jesus.
- I am in Christ now. I am in Christ. I am in Christ. Amen.
- Lord, transfuse my blood with the Blood of Jesus.

I repent for the sins of my ancestors. And for my own marriage violations, Lord, forgive me, I repent. Lord, cover them all with the Blood of Jesus. Amen.

- Battles of offended *gods* in my life, die by the power in the Blood of Jesus.
- Strongman at the gate of my marriage, be bound and then die, in the Name of Jesus. the King of Glory is coming in, in the Name of Jesus. Amen.

Ruth was a widow, a Moabitess, but she was still redeemed. She had a Kinsman Redeemer, Boaz. No matter what foundation we have, no matter what bloodline we've been born into, no matter how bad we were before we got to Christ, Jesus is our Kinsman Redeemer. If we appropriate Christ, we can be redeemed.

Ask

Ask for and get sexual rights to have a legal Kingdom spouse. You must ask and you must ask the right person. You don't just take things, or do whatever you want and then believe that you have a legal Kingdom spouse.

Even if legally married you can't have relations with your spouse, without punishment, and without judgment unless you have the sexual rights of the person (woman) that you are married to. Once you have those rights, you get to enjoy your spouse. You get to enjoy your marriage. You get to be fruitful and multiply and bring forth righteous seed. Anything else is perversion.

Just getting busy with somebody without permission or even *with* consent of the individual you're getting busy with is not all it takes. Especially since the Me-Too Movement, the world is very busy insisting that the woman, especially must give her *consent*. But does she even have consent to give? Who holds and maintains the sexual rights of a girl? Of a woman? Who?

No, you have got to follow proper godly channels because if not, you're not going to get the **blessing** in that relationship. You may call it a marriage, but **it's not a marriage unless God says it is**. What God puts together; no man can break apart.

Sex creates the covenant; if the marriage is not consummated, the couple is not married. Sex covenant needs God in it. A righteous covenant needs God in it or else, by default, the devil or any of his *idol gods* or his demons will automatically get in it. Satan is the prince of this world; he is everywhere you **<u>don't</u>** want him to be, unless you are prayed up and keeping him out of your life, your sex life, especially, and out of your marriage.

Sex is a vow, and it consummates marriage. A Kingdom marriage can bring forth Kingdom kids and righteous seeds. Fornication and adultery bring on the Curse of the Law. *Goes into* equals married.

> And if a man entices a maiden that he is not betrothed to, and he lies with her, he shall surely endow her to be his wife,
> (Exodus, 22:16).

After the *deed*, that man may swear, or may say, that she gave consent, but, of course, it wasn't his to take, but was it hers to give? The question becomes then, what are the *gods* of that woman's house, or that woman's father's house that she is subject to that may be claiming her sexual and reproductive rights even before she was born?

This is why we do the deep foundational work and deliverance before marriage, to marry, to stay married, and to enjoy our marriages, and to be fruitful and multiply.

The ONLY way to avoid this is if this woman is not subject to any idol *gods*. That means she's fully delivered and she's in Christ. And if a person is fully in Christ, then who can give her consent? The sexual consent and permission now comes from God, because God only gives legal sexual rights and marriage. Anything else is disobedience and a perversion.

Any of us may say, we have no idols, You don't serve any idol *gods* or *goddesses*. But if you're a member of any secret society, or if your father, mother, ancestors were Freemasons, Eastern Star, Shriners, or if you or them were in any fraternity, any sorority--, any secret society, then you are somehow connected to, and possibly betrothed or married to idol *gods*, just by the oaths and the vows that you've made in those secret societies. Worse, you may not even know it.

Frat boys are famous for running about chasing women. And they think they're having fun, but they may not be able to stop because it could be built into the covenant that they have with the idol *gods* and goddesses of their fraternity that they won't marry, and they'll just chase skirt forever.

You had better dig deep to find out if you are in allegiance with these idol *gods*, which they are and how to extricate yourself from them.

If you are already married or betrothed to idol *gods* and goddesses--, that could be one of the reasons you're not married today.

You may be thinking, oh, you'll just do it on your own. You'll just take your chances. You're like, oh it's my body, it's my life. Well, if you're saved, your body belongs to Christ. If you're married, your body belongs to your spouse. So, is it your body? Your life?

That's how the world talks. But if you're in Christ, you need to consult with God. You need to consult the Word of God. To see what is legal and what is expedient for your life.

Masturbation is Unauthorized

Masturbation is giving your sexual rights away to *Nobody*. You may be thinking that you're the only one present--, but you are not. Folks, you are never alone the entire time you are alive on this planet. If you're good there are guardian angels round about you. If you're bad there are guardian demons, *monitoring spirits, familiar spirits* and such like. You are never alone.

Now, knowing that, let's revisit the above statement: Masturbation is you giving your sexual rights to *Nobody*. *Nobody* is a demon. *Nobody* is a demon who has named himself, *Nobody*.

This is unauthorized use of sexual organs and reproductive rights, and God hates spilled seed. Onan was killed for that.

But let's talk about *Nobody* some more. If you're currently married to *Nobody*, which is a demon because of all the sexual consummation you've done with the demon, *Nobody* present, this could be why you're not married today. In the spirit you are married to *Nobody* and in the natural world, you are also married to *Nobody*.

Nobody may not be the actual name that the demon has selected, but on deliverance ground one may have occasion to ask a demon it's name, and *Nobody* has been a name bandied about during deliverances. However, the name could be *Anybody*. It could be *Somebody*. It could be *The Man, The Dude, The Boss*. Whatever a demon thinks up and calls himself, he could call himself *Prince Charming,* but he's still a demon.

With the other gender, on the other hand, the spiritual entity could be a female incubus named anything: *Princess, Snow White, Cinderella*. While in the act, whatever you're conjuring up or looking at while you do the deed, that's what you're married to, or the image of something, but there is a demon behind it, or charging it to attract and keep your attention.

Nobody--, the demon called, *Nobody* has your sexual rights. Aside from your potential Kingdom spouse not being able to **see** you because your glory is either taken or covered. If they could see you, they may not even see you as available because you've got that married already vibe about you. This could be why you're not married today.

That's bad enough, but it's worse if you have an actual human spouse, but you're cheating on that spouse with **Nobody** and **Nobody** has captured your sexual rights, because you offered them up, and your human spouse is no longer interesting to you. That's what happens with unauthorized use of your body that is vowed to your marriage partner.

Nobody has become your *spirit spouse* even though you are married and living in the same house with your human spouse, but you're on the couch or in the guest bedroom most nights. Don't let this be you.

Spirit spouse is a **spiritual** problem created by the spiritual crime (sin) of unauthorized use. This spiritual problem cannot be solved in the natural by your spouse losing weight or becoming "hotter." No matter who created the spiritual error, deliverance is needed so you all can be free of this spirit spouse and be strong in the Lord resisting backsliding into unauthorized use of the sexual organs.

What's done in the dark will be uncovered in the light. What you did when you thought you were alone, and the bathroom door was locked – oh please. No one is ever alone.

Marriage is the only way to legally give and transfer sexual rights and reproductive rights.

If God joins two people together, then why does the marriage end up being torment or torture, even rocky? Because they were idol *gods* of the Father's houses that are rioting, offended outraged, demanding loyalty and worship from its subjects.

Marriage vows are made in front of a preacher or other officiant. Especially if in a church, why are all these different levels of idolatry involved leading up to walking down the aisle, if the vows are made to God? If God is offended by idolatry, then is God even <u>at</u> the wedding? What God has joined together, let no man put asunder. And I ask again, is God even *at* this wedding? Is God involved in whatever's happening in this church, or at the beach or in a forest or in a barn or wherever you're doing this?

Be sure that you, your spouse and your marriage are all in Christ, so this can be remedied.

When idols have authority, or believe they have authority over you or your spouse or both of you they will wreak havoc in your marriage. It depends on your culture. Depends on your background and traditions you come from. Depends on if you've been dedicated to some unknown entity or not. It depends on your own thousand Oaths that you previously made in secret societies, or just to your friends and passing, just saying things that you thought were clever, silly, or fun and they weren't any of that. Instead, they were spiritually dangerous words you may have spoken.

It depends on if you have soul ties, If you already have spirit marriages, depends on if you were *entertaining* yourself and conjuring up things. This could be why you're not married today.

So, what about a person who was married and now they're divorced? Can they marry again? What happens to those sexual rights? Who has those? Well, a widow or properly divorced person, woman, man, who is saved, God needs to be consulted before that person can enter again into marriage. If she has no male relatives alive, according to tradition to approve of her getting married, she has her own sexual rights. We all need to be sure that when we're making a wedding vow, or any kind of vow that we fulfill them, especially those to the Lord.

If we're getting into a marriage – first second--, any marriage, be sure that God is fully in it. God. Just God, not a bunch of idol *gods* based on superstitions and cultural traditions. The righteous exchange of vows makes for a Kingdom marriage, and that's what will bring forth Kingdom kids, righteous seed. Amen.

So, your job is to protect your own children, your own child, until they can protect themselves. You need to protect their sexual rights spiritually. They are under your guard and your authority. Protect your child's sexual rights until they are of age themselves, and spiritually accountable.

As said, *evil spirit marriage* can result from any type of unauthorized sex with a known or unknown spiritual entity or physical person. It could be with a spiritual entity masquerading as or having jumped in a physical person.

Even if you are alone and masturbating, no matter what a demon calls itself --, *Nobody, Somebody, Mr. Dude-,* porn star online--, whatever it's called, it is an enemy. It always is an enemy to your soul. We should never marry an enemy in the spirit or in the natural.

Sex Magic

Sex magic is conjuring up and agreeing with a demon, while having sex or doing something sexual in exchange for something you want or something you think you want. You end up married to that demon and you may or may not get that thing that you want. That's one type of *spirit spouse*. How do you plan to get rid of it?

Then there's blind witchcraft. If someone told you what to say at some certain time in the sex act, if they knew what they were doing, suspect sex magic. Of course, they could just be lewd and loud and have no idea of what they were doing. If neither of you know, maybe there's two blind witches--, but it is still sex magic because at least one of you is unauthorized and both of you are doing things that you know not of--, unauthorized things. Fantasy role play is dangerous because it invites demons. Ungodly activities in the bedroom, by any other name, it is still sex magic.

Any witchcraft is unauthorized use of power if you are saved and in Christ. Any witchcraft in the bedroom, especially is sex magic.

Sexual curiosity, especially in the immature, can cause a person to give their sexual rights away, unknowingly.

Soul ties are created by experiences that a person is probably too emotionally and/or spiritually immature to handle. We shouldn't have all these sexual experiences because this is why people are still thinking about that first time or that first one. They are soul tied.

Dr. Frederick Hightower, said one of the most interesting things many years ago, and I can't forget it. He said. *A person's first sexual experience colors what their sexual proclivity will be for the rest of their life.*

In that same conversation, he described a pornsexual and describe them as people who are not satisfied unless they're chasing or using porn. And in so doing, that person, (I'm adding this part), is scattering their sexual rights all over the place. Porn-oholics may or may not be surprised to know that porn sets are satanic, there are pentagrams and other evil images, chants, rituals and requirements going on to get the actors to do all the stuff they do for the camera. When you watch it, participate in it, like it – you too are worshipping Satan just as they are.

Neither Satan nor satanic worship should ever be in a sex covenant with a person who confesses Christ.

Worshipping Satan in any way captures, diminishes or covers your star. Your marriage and other good things are in your star, but if your star is stolen, it could be why you are not married today. Divine connections that should be in your star didn't happen and it could be why you're not married. Marriage is a divine appointment.

The marriage vow is very serious. It is until death do us part. Every *to the death* vow is heavy. Death of the star can happen in the hands of evil star hunters. **Death of sexual rights could lead to the death of a marriage**.

Onan was trying to take Tamar's sexual rights without committing to her; God struck him dead.

King David sent for Bathsheba and took her sexual rights. Then he had her husband Uriah killed so he could keep those rights. Then David and Bathsheba's first born died.

Sexual and reproductive rights are serious, they are no joking matter.

If you are not married, or if you're not happily married right now, today, it could be because sexual rights are not in your possession or under your control.

If some *entity* has control of your sexual rights, it has taken the enjoyment out of your marriage. This could be ruining a whole marriage right now.

If sexual rights are lost, the restoration of them takes deliverance. That overprotective man who is now the father of a newborn baby girl rises up to say maybe without realizing it that he will protect her until a man that's good enough for her comes along. He may not know it, but he means he will protect her sexual rights.

But somewhere in the course of that little girl growing up to a teen and then a young woman, does he forget? Does he get tired? Does he get deceived and tricked by Satan? Unless dad or if there is only one parent gives authorization, any sex that girl has is unauthorized. And the man she has sex with is also UNAUTHORIZED and under all curses and penalties that go with that.

Both of Lot's daughters became pregnant by their father which we have learned is Satanic. The older daughter had a son named Moab; he's the father of the Moabites. Remember, Ruth was a Moabitess. The younger daughter had a son, and she named him Ben Ami. He is the father of the Ammonites.

God wasn't in this plan that Lot's daughters cooked up. God wasn't in that emotional, evil, satanic, flesh decision of the girls taking advantage of their drunk father, when they got him drunk two nights in a row and accessed unauthorized use of his reproductive system.

In so doing, these two girls gave their sexual rights to demons. No, they didn't give it back to the father because if they were virgins, the father was already in custody of, and supposedly protecting their sexual rights, until they married. But those two girls gave their sexual rights to demons. I say that because God wasn't in those transactions--, neither of those transactions, and neither of those girls. Neither of their children were righteous seed because it would have been impossible for them to be righteous seed even though the daughters may have had good intentions. Some **unauthorized use** is so perverse that there is no way that God can even get in it, especially when it is dreamed up by evil or ignorant people.

The Moabites worshipped false *gods*, and they're known for sexual immorality. They worshipped Chemosh. And the Ammonites? They are evil as well. They worship Molech, who was particularly evil in the Bible. He was the testable Molech demanded child sacrifice. And this practice is strictly forbidden in Mosaic Law and in our times too.

I Said It's Golden

This is why the devil requires those who worship him, to violate their own. It's to take their sexual rights, which is heinous and grievous to God. Many of them marry their daughters off to someone or *something* foul and disgusting, taking her sexual rights, so it's no longer available for a normal marriage. In essence, this evil person is selling her sexual rights for some desired thing that *he* wants. Fame, success, money.

It's not just men who do this. An evil, witchy or occultic mother could do this as well. And this often leaves daughters confused, wondering why they are not married. Why haven't they had any suitors? Hasn't their father approved of any of the suitors that they have had, if they've had any? It could be because he doesn't want them married or he's already sold off their sexual rights.

Again, it doesn't have to be a parent or an older person who causes the loss of sexual rights.

Carelessness and adolescence can lead to the loss of glory, the loss of a star, and the loss of sexual rights.

Jacob dared steal the birthright from his brother Esau, but he didn't dare violate marital or sexual rights protocol with regards to Rachel. Laban had a watchful eye over his daughters.

New dads of little girls, I charge you to keep up the enthusiasm of protecting your daughter's chastity. Yes, be protective of her, but you can't do that in the flesh. The way you protect your daughter, her flesh, her soul, and her spirit is in the spirit. You protect her sexual rights in prayer, in spiritual warfare, from birth, or even before. You protect her sexual rights by having a right foundation yourself. Keeping yourself right before God. Saved. Delivered, prayed up. You protect your daughter's sexual rights by having a right relationship with her mother and both of you together make sure both of your ancestral foundations are right before God so no evil can creep in.

Teach your daughters right from wrong. You model to them in action what a proper husband is by the way you treat their mother. Yes, their other parent is part of their upbringing and

God is fully in the picture. This is how you protect your daughter's sexual rights from being stolen, taken, or being given away to some smooth talker or a thug.

Just as Esau didn't put value on his birthright, people don't put value on their sexual rights, if they aren't taught what it is, how important it is, and how to protect those rights. Unprotected sexual rights could lead to marital disaster or no marriage at all.

Dads, you know--, men are out there sowing wild oats. Sexual rights are not oats. But there's this man who's out there scattering his own sexual rights while he's also stealing rights from others. And this is what promiscuous people are doing, scattering themselves all about town, all about the world, doing unauthorized sexual things.

If they adopt the devil's playboy mentality disaster looms. There's nothing to play about, this is too serious. Random sex leads to health problems, poverty, soul ties, *spirit spouse*, polygamy, witchcraft, dissensions, fights, gossip, wars—every work of the flesh.

It takes away the glory of those involved, while you're being ripped off. The enemies are stealing from you, stealing your ideas, your breakthroughs. It can lead to barrenness, and infertility in the natural.

Random sex in the natural gets the same results as sex in the dream. In the dream it is having sex with a demon. In the natural, you don't know what demons are on board the person you may randomly hook up with. The last seven of theirs swaps out with the last seven that you picked up. It's gross, so gross.

Remember, **Nobody** is a demon. It could be multiple demons. It's not always just one. Are you having sex with somebody in your imagination? The devil will gladly listen in or send a *monitoring spirit* to listen in to see what you like and form a weapon against you.

In the world, swipers are swiping sexual rights and the swipe-ees have themselves out there on the auction block, selling **what's golden** for no money. No money. Neither answer is acceptable, giving it away for free or selling it, but there they are sinning against their own body and working corruption into their own lives.

How can a couple bring forth righteous seed if both are defiled before the marriage?

- Lord, in the Name of Jesus, any entity, power or idol requiring that I do anything ungodly to be approved for marriage, fall down and die, in the Name of Jesus. I am in Christ.

No matter what you've done or been through, the Lord can save you. Anyone who used to worship false *gods* can be saved if they turn from that to the Lord Jesus Christ. Amen.

A harlot can be saved.

A man who cannot be satisfied with one woman is not only a man, but he is also a man with demons, multiple demons, most likely. The more that man seeks to be satisfied with multiple women, the more demons he picks up. Then he's driven into the streets to try to satisfy these demons, which he thinks are his *own* desires. But it is the *lust* of the demons that he's trying to satisfy.

All hope is not lost; there is deliverance. This person needs deliverance so he can become **one** man again and be satisfied with **one** woman which is his charge from the book of Genesis to be fruitful and multiply in the context of marriage.

Unless You Are In Christ

If you are not in Christ and you want to get married, you could have to appease more than a hundred marriage deities, depending on where you are born and live in the world. As well, the numbers of marriage deities in your marriage also depends on the culture of the person that you are marrying.

Unless you are in Christ, and then you can override all of it. But that means you have to be **fully** in Christ, fully put on, and appropriate Christ, or these idol *gods* of your father's house, even of your mother's house. These idol *gods* that you may have invoked by your own choices, your own sins can interfere in your getting married. So, if there are idol *gods* in your foundation or in your bloodline, from your father's house or your mother's house, and if they ever got worship from your ancestors down your bloodline, if they ever got worship and they're not getting it now, they may put up barriers to you getting married.

This could be why you're not married right now. This could be why you are married, but not happily married right now. Whatever is in a family bloodline by the 3rd generation, it's **really** in there. It's really in there. To get them out, you're going to need Christ; He is your only salvation, the only way out.

More men than I care to mention seem to think that women are interchangeable. And they are not. Sometimes men get married by timing. When they think it's *time* to get married, then whoever comes along, that's who they marry. So that's not in my Bible.

But saints of God there are strongmen at the Gate of your marriage and that's probably why you are not married today. There is a Marital Gate and barriers have been erected by idol *gods* and strongholds and guarded over by a strongman. Uh--, and you thought to stay single was your idea. It wasn't. You need to be spiritually discerning and aware to know this, however, or you can be deceived your entire life.

Marriage requirements that you may know nothing about may have been set up by your culture, by traditions, by your bloodline, by your place of birth, by your place of residence, where you live right now. Do you even have permission from the *territorial spirits* to be in that place where you are to work, to live, or to find a spouse there? If not, you need Christ, that is the only way you will override this.

How do you know that you don't have permission? Things aren't working out for you there--, like at all. Not in work, career, relationships, friendships, or marriage. Did you pray before entering that city? Well, no wonder.

So, there are strongmen at these gates, and these strongmen work for the devil, and they're at that gate to keep you from entering in. Through the gate of your marriage is a strong room, or inside is a territory or land that belongs to you— a Promised Land. Strongmen must be removed and taken down.

> Lift up your heads, you gates;
> be lifted up, you ancient doors,
> that the King of glory may come in.
> Who is this King of glory?
> The LORD strong and mighty,
> the LORD mighty in battle.
> Lift up your heads, you gates;
> lift them up, you ancient doors,
> that the King of glory may come in.
> Who is he, this King of glory?
> The LORD Almighty—
> he is the King of glory. (Psalm 24:7-10)

So, this is the gate of your breakthrough. It needs to lift up its head. It needs to be lifted up so the King of Glory can come in through the Gate of your marriage.

The requirements at the Marriage Gate of these marriage deities are associated with romance and love and lust, virility, fertility, and sex, mostly. They are there to declare if the person you want to marry and the season and reason you want to marry is okay or not. They want to give or revoke authorization. Some of these deities rule over beauty and luxury, and that is why so many spend so much on weddings and honeymoons, even breaking the bank. The *gods* are demanding it and the humans may not even know why they are spending like crazy or doing outrageous things for their nuptials. They just know they have got to have things a certain way. Uh huh.

If you are in Christ, He is the only one and His Word says if you are authorized or not to enter into relationships, marriage, sex and reproductive activities.

If and when you gave away your virginity, you gave away a lot more than you think, a lot more than you realize, and entangled yourself and your sexual rights with the enemy. This invites *spirit spouse* and any demon that hangs around you believes it is married to you. Fornication, masturbation and any other kind of illicit sex, adultery--, any type of sex where you're not married and, in a God,-recognized marriage covenant and you're have relations with that person is illicit sex. Just one unauthorized person in a sexual situation can bring on the demons, and this could be why you're not married today, even though you have dated many people, and may even have one or more baby momma's or baby daddies. Unauthorized sexual use creates iniquity and spiritual problems for you, your spouse, your marriage and your children.

Now you are entering into a whole different evil covenant. You're creating soul ties. God's not in it. So that means that the prince of this world can send in anybody he wants to, he can send in any *Nobody*. This begins the battles for your sexual rights, unless it had already started by evil inheritance down ancestral lines.

Any of us may be surprised at how many teenagers are having sex in the dream and telling absolutely no one about it. This is an attack for that child's sexual rights, and the battle over reproductive rights.

The *spirit of the player* is driven by *lust* as we said, and it is an anti-marital curse. It's an anti-marital *spirit*. An anti-marital curse can be sent to a person by evil human agents that work for the devil on the Earth. A cheating spouse is an anti-marriage curse with evil *spirits*. And that they are all driven by *lust*.

There are anti-marriage spells out here operating against Godly marriages. So why are the battles to get married and stay married so intense? Witchcraft and anti-marriage spells. That means you might be a person who can't even find a mate, find a suitor, or a spouse.

Or if you do find one then something ridiculous happens, something crazy or maybe even tragic happens, so the marriage doesn't take place. There are spells for marital breakups, marriage, marriage failures. All of this is out there, people, and you've gotta stay prayed up. And if you don't believe in spells, well, you don't have to believe in spells. The person casting the spell is the person who is to believe in them. You pray to God, right? Well, you believe in God and others don't, but God still moves on your behalf. And it's not dependent upon what you believe in, unless you are fully in Christ, and you believe that the enemy's spells can't touch you because you are prayed up.

- Lord, in the Name of Jesus, whatever I'm supposed to have, including the Kingdom spouse that I don't have, Blood of Jesus pay for me, in the Name of Jesus.
- All battles of violated marriage rituals by my parents and ancestors, Lord, for the sake of Christ, release my sexual rights in marriage and let me fulfill destiny, in the Name of Jesus.
- My sexual rights in the grip of darkness, I take it back. I take it back. I take it back--, in the Name of Jesus.
- Every manipulation of my sexual rights be stopped, in the Name of Jesus.
- Lord, every unnatural decrease or increase in libido, normalize it now, in the Name of Jesus.
- Flesh and blood, taking orders from darkness, die, in the Name of Jesus.
- Flesh and blood taking orders to delay, stop, or destroy my marriage, Cease and desist in the Name of Jesus.
- Powers that will not allow me to be married, stay married, or be happy and married, die, in the Name of Jesus.

- Arise O Lord, judge the idols that are against my destiny. Water, air and land made them, in the Name of Jesus.
- I break the agreement by the power in the Blood of Jesus.
- Powers sitting on my soul and not getting my worship and you are punishing me, die, and let your punishment die and backfire, in the Name of Jesus.
- Powers in my soul there to block my ears so I don't hear God, die so I can hear God, in the Name of Jesus.
- Lord, in the Name of Jesus, uncurse me, uncurse me, uncurse my ring finger, in the Name of Jesus

You put on Christ and appropriate Christ you can be saved and delivered and used mightily of God. Salmon and Rahab, Boaz, Obed, Jessee Matthew 1:5

Rahab, who was a harlot is one of 5 women mentioned in the genealogy of Christ. Tamar, Rahab, Ruth, Bathsheba, and Mary the mother of Jesus. Other than Mary, Rahab is the only one mentioned again in the New Testament; there is no condemnation in Christ Jesus. So, if He saves you, even if you were the worst sinner doing all manner of unauthorized sexual stuff out here in these streets, you are saved and made clean and purified and made whole again, in the Name of Jesus.

Whom the Son sets free is free, indeed.

Excluding Mary, of those 4 women, which one was perfect before coming to the kingdom? Tell me which one. So you take a moment and let the Love and Mercy of God wash over you, because if God can use and accept those women and wash away their sins even in the lineage of Jesus Christ, then cleaning you up and redeeming you from your own transgressions is EASY for God. Nothing is impossible for God and He will do it if you ask Him.

- Let the sacrifice of Christ pay for me.
- Lift up your head. Oh ye gates.
- Powers at the gate of my next level breakthrough, you are robbers and destroyers; fall down and die, in the Name of Jesus.
- Holy Spirit, You are the Minister of Deliverance; fall on these prayers today in the Name of Jesus.
- Lord, I repent for the sins, my own sins, and the sins of my ancestors.

- May the Blood of Jesus wash over us.
- Cover us, Lord, with the Blood of Jesus.
- Lord, thank You for the authority to pray these prayers, in Jesus' Name.
- Lord, if I am single, put my name in the register of those who are available to be married. And do not send any inappropriate suitors to me, in the Name of Jesus. Lord, block every unacceptable and inappropriate suitor that the enemy may send, in the Name of Jesus.
- In the Name of Jesus, Lord, I reject every adversary. I reject every enemy. Lord, send me a like-minded soul mate--, not a roommate, not a jail mate, in the Name of Jesus.
- Lord, send me a communicator, one who says what they mean in truth and in love, and one who hears me when I speak. So that we are mutually respectful of one another.
- Lord, send a suitor who wants to get married. Someone like minded first having their mind on you and then on marriage on building and fulfilling destiny, not someone I have to urge or talk into matrimony, in the Name of Jesus.

- Strong men at the gate of my marital breakthrough, be bound and removed by mighty warrior angels of God.
- Any authority that stands in the way of my marriage be defeated, in the Name of Jesus.
- In the Name of the Lord, let every weapon used against my marriage backfire.
- Lord Jesus, call my Kingdom spouse to me and me to my Kingdom spouse today, in the Name of Jesus.
- Lord, make Your perfect will for my marriage plain to me, in the Name of Jesus.
- Lord, bless me to do Your will and Your purpose now and after marriage, in the Name of Jesus.
- In this marriage battle, Lord, let me be fruitful in the Name of Jesus.
- Idols in my soul sponsoring self-destruction, destroy yourselves, in the Name of Jesus.
- Evil entities hovering over my destiny be cut off by the power in the Blood of Jesus.
- Any evil prophecy causing me to cry in secret be silenced by the power in the Blood of Jesus.

- Idols in my soul, taking worship by my suffering, die by the power in the Blood of Jesus.
- Serpent of the Lord that are speaking when the Holy Spirit must speak when Jesus Christ must speak, the Lord rebuke you. Be quiet; shut up, in the Name of Jesus.
- Any voices that would speak to me in the place of God; the Lord Jesus rebuke you, shut up and die out of my soul.
- In the Name of Jesus, Lord, clear my soul of distractions within me that cloud my ears or my brain.
- And the same I ask for my intended, my intended Kingdom spouse, in the Name of Jesus.
- Battles of the *gods* in my life showing up as backward dreams, die by the power in the Blood of Jesus.
- Powers and idols that used marriage to torment my parents and ancestors, and you're still at work in my life, the Lord Jesus rebuke you, in the Name of Jesus.
- By the power of the Blood of Jesus, battles that kicked my ancestors out of marriage

and are still ongoing, die with your sponsors out of my soul.
- By the power of the Blood of Jesus, I repent, Lord, of all the sins of ancestral and idol worship in my bloodline, in the Name of Jesus.
- Lord, I repent of all unauthorized use that I have committed against me, or allowed to be committed on my person, in the Name of Jesus.
- Lord have Mercy upon me for the unauthorized use that I disallowed, but I was forced into, in the Name of Jesus.
- Power in the Blood of Jesus, I *loose* myself from curses, from spells, from the enchantment, from idolatry, vexes, hexes and jinxes, of my father's house, in the Name of Jesus.
- By the power in the Blood of Jesus, I loose myself from the curses of exes, fake friends, and evil associates, in the Name of Jesus.
- Everything that I've done to offend, insult, or interfere in anyone else's marriage, knowingly or unknowingly, Lord, I repent, *in the Name of Yeshua.*

- Lord, wash me with the Blood of Jesus; create in me a clean heart. Amen.
- Any marriage punishment that I have coming, Lord, have Mercy and remove that punishment, in the Name of Jesus.
- Ancient idols, in my foundation, die, in the Name of Jesus.
- All oppositions and oppression coming from the altars of the idols of my Father's house, I challenge you with the power and the Blood of Jesus, die, in the Name of Jesus.
- Idolatry in my foundation manifesting through food, die, in the Name of Jesus.
- Idolatry in my blood manifesting through obedience to anti-Kingdom traditions and cultures, die, in the Name of Jesus.

Marriage is not with or to the *gods* of my father's house. My marriage is not with or to the *gods* of my father's house. My marriage is not with or *to* the *gods* of my father's house. My marriage is not with or to the *gods* of my father's house. I decommission every idolatrous requirement for marriage from my father's house.

- I decommission every ideological knowledge from my father's house, in the Name of Jesus.
- Battles of violated marriage rituals by my parents and ancestors for the sake of Christ, Lord release my marriage and let me fulfill destiny, in the Name of Jesus.
- Jesus, You are the only one who can fix this. For the sake of Christ, release me now. Release me now. Release me now in the Name of Jesus.

Agenda to have me to never breakthrough until I perform a dark ritual, Backfire, Backfire, backfire and let me fulfill destiny, in the Name of Yeshua.

Agenda of strange altars of my father's house or my mother's house backfire and let me fulfill destiny.

Agenda to have me never breakthrough until I worship family idols even though I am in Christ, die, in the Name of Jesus.

Anti-marriage agendas of my native place, backfire, in the Name of Jesus.

Agenda to have me never breakthrough until I obey family idols, backfire, in the Name of Jesus.

If my blood is shouting that I am not a woman, I have nothing to prove by unauthorized use of my womanhood, I reject the temptation now, in the Name of Jesus.

If my blood is shouting that I am not a man, I have nothing to prove by unauthorized use of my manhood, I reject the temptation and the provocation now, in the Name of Jesus Christ.

I silence every evil voice with that of Jesus. If your blood is crying out against you, but you are now in Christ, silence that voice, with the Blood of Jesus. If your blood is shouting that you are not a man, and you are, and you are now in Christ, silence that voice with the Blood of Jesus.

Silence that voice with the blood of Jesus.

Attacks because of these prayers, these decrees and deliverance, backfire seven times, in the Name of Jesus. (several times)

I seal these prayers, decrees, and declarations across every realm, timeline, and dimension, past, present, and future, to Infinity, in the Name of Jesus, by the Blood of Jesus, and by the Holy Spirit of Promise.

Thank You, Lord Jesus. I count this as done.

Amen.

Dear Reader:

Thank you for acquiring and reading this book. I pray it has been a blessing to you and will change how you see and do things, spiritually, for the better.

May God help the custodian of your sexual rights maintain them appropriately until your marriage if you are single. If you are married, may you and your spouse maintain and protect both your sexual rights, and give God the glory in your relationship.

I pray you all have Wisdom, discernment, and resistance against any and all Unauthorized use of your person, in the Name of Jesus.

In the Name of Jesus,

AMEN.

Dr. Marlene Miles

Other books by this author

AK: The Adventures of the Agape Kid

AMONG SOME THIEVES

Ancestral Powers

Backstabbers

Barrenness, *Prayers Against*
https://a.co/d/feUtIs

Battlefield of Marriage, *The*

Beauty Curses, *Warfare Prayers Against*
https://a.co/d/5Xlc20M

Blindsided: *Has the Old Man Bewitched You?*

https://a.co/d/5O2fLLR

Break Free from Collective Captivity

Casting Down Imaginations

Churchzilla, The Wanna-Be, Supposed-to-be Bride of Christ

Courts of Marriage: Prayers for Marriage in the Courts of Heaven (prayerbook)

Courtroom Warfare @ Midnight (prayerbook)

Curses of Blind Men

Demonic Cobwebs (prayerbook)

Demonic Time Bombs

Demons Hate Questions

Devil Loves Trauma, *The*

Devil Weapons: Unforgiveness, Bitterness,…

The Devourers: Thieves of Darkness 2

Do Not Swear by the Moon

Don't Refuse Me, Lord (4 book series)
https://a.co/d/idP34LG

Dream Defilement

The Emptiers: *Thieves of Darkness, 1*
https://a.co/d/5I4n5mc

Every Evil Bird

Evil Touch

Failed Assignment

Fantasy Spirit Spouse https://a.co/d/hW7oYbX

FAT Demons (The): *Breaking Demonic Curses*

The Fold (5-book series)

- The Fold (Book 1)
- Name Your Seed (Book 2)
- The Poor Attitudes of Money (3)
- Do Not Orphan Your Seed (4)
- For the Sake of the Gospel (5)
- My Sowing Journal

Fruit of the Womb: *Prayers Against Barrenness*

Gang Ups: Touch Not God's Anointed

Gates of Thanksgiving

got HEALING? Verses for Life

got LOVE? Verses for Life

got HOPE? Verses for Life

got money? https://a.co/d/g2av41N

How to Dental Assist

How to Dental Assit2: Be Productive, Not Wasteful

I Take It Back

Legacy

Let Me Have A Dollar's Worth
https://a.co/d/h8F8XgE

Level the Playing Field

Living for the NOW of God

Lose My Location https://a.co/d/crD6mV9

Man Safari, *The*

Marriage Ed. Rules of Engagement & Marriage

Made Perfect in Love

Money Hunters: Beware of Those

Money on the Altar https://a.co/d/4EqJ2Nr

Mulberry Tree https://a.co/d/9nR9rRb

Motherboard (The) - *Soul Prosperity Series*

Name Your Seed

Occupy: *Until I Return*

Plantation Souls

Players Gonna Play

Power Money: Nine Times the Tithe

https://a.co/d/gRt41gy

The Power of Wealth *(forthcoming)*

Powers Above

The Robe, Part 1, The Lessons of Joseph

The Robe, Part II, The Lessons of Joseph

Seasons of Grief

Seasons of Waiting

Seasons of War

Second Marriage, Third--, Any Marriage

Sift You Like Wheat

Six Men Short: What Has Happened to all the Men?

Spirits of Death, Hell & the Grave, Pass Over Me and My House

Soul Prosperity soul prosperity series 3

https://a.co/d/5p8YvCN

Souls Captivity soul prosperity series 2

The Spirit of Poverty

StarStruck

SUNBLOCK

The Swallowers: *Thieves of Darkness*, 3

Take It Back

This Is NOT That: How to Keep Demons from Coming at You

Throne of Grace: Courtroom Prayer

Time Is of the Essence

Too Many Wives: *Why You Have Lady Problems*

Tormenting Spirits   https://a.co/d/dAogEJf

Toxic Souls

Triangular Power *(series)*

- Powers Above
- SUNBLOCK
- Do Not Swear by the Moon
- STARSTRUCK

Uncontested Doom

Unguarded Hours, *The*

Unseen Life, *The* (forthcoming)

Upgrade: How to Get Out of Survival Mode

- Toxic Souls (Book 2 of series)

- Legacy (Book 3 of series)

Warfare Prayer Against Beauty Curses

Warfare Prayer Against Poverty
https://a.co/d/bZ61lYu

The Wasters: *Thieves of Darkness*, Bk 2
https://a.co/d/bUvI9Jo

What Have You to Declare? What Do You Have With You from Where You've Been?

When I Was A Child, *I Prayed As a Child*

When the Devourer is Rebuked

https://a.co/d/1HVv8oq

The Wilderness Romance *(series)* This series is about conducting a Godly relationship and marriage with someone who is a Wilderness person. It is about how to recognize it and navigate through it. These books are about how not to get caught up in such.

- *The Social Wilderness*
- *The Sexual Wilderness*
- *The Spiritual Wilderness*

Other Series

The Fold (a series on Godly finances)
https://a.co/d/4hz3unj

Soul Prosperity Series https://a.co/d/bz2M42q

Spirit Spouse books

https://a.co/d/9VehDSo

https://a.co/d/97sKOwm

Thieves of Darkness series

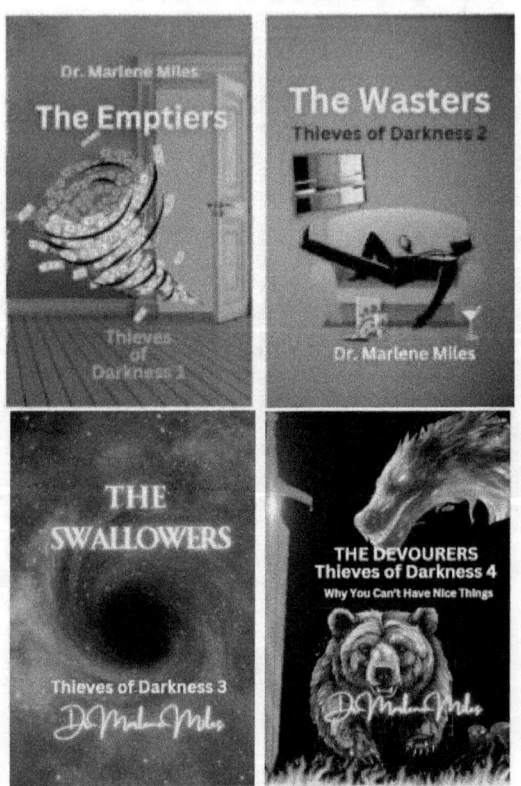

Triangular Powers https://a.co/d/aUCjAWC

Upgrade (series) *How to Get Out of Survival Mode*
https://a.co/d/aTERhXO

Credits

Prayers mostly by Pastor Dr. Anthony Akerele

Mountain of Fire Ministries, *The gods and Your Needs*
https://www.youtube.com/watch?v=gmNKpAppqTo

www.ingramcontent.com/pod-product-compliance
Lightning Source LLC
LaVergne TN
LVHW021407080426
835508LV00020B/2481